PLAN FOR SUCCESS

Other Books by James R. Sherman

How to Overcome a Bad Back

Rejection

Get Set . . . GO!

Middle Age Is Not A Disease

Escape to the Gunflint

•

In the **DO IT!** Series

Stop Procrastinating—DO IT!

Patience Pays Off

No More Mistakes

Farewell To Fear

Be A Winner

PLAN FOR SUCCESS

James R. Sherman

Pathway Books

First Edition, May, 1989
Copyright © 1989 James R. Sherman
All Rights Reserved

Library of Congress Catalog Number
87-062619

International Standard Book Number
0-935538-12-7

Printed in the United States of America

Pathway Books
700 Parkview Terrace
Golden Valley, Minnesota 55416
(612) 377-1521

To: The Elderberries

Marilyn and Art
Marge and Doug
Thea and Fred
Laura and Al

CONTENTS

PLAN OF ACTION

PREFACE

On your mark . . .
Get set . . .
Get set . . .
Get set . . .

A lot of people who find themselves in the competitive scramble for success never get out of the starting blocks.

They're frustrated, because no matter what they do, they just can't seem to get ahead. They go to workshops, retreats, and seminars to feel better about themselves. They read all the motivational material they can get their hands on. And they try to do the things that successful people do. Sometimes they can see themselves as being successful people, but that's about as far as they get.

I've been frustrated that way myself. My expectations of success usually lasted a week or so. And then I'd find myself back in the same old rut of not knowing what to do next.

It wasn't that I didn't want to get better at what I was doing, or that I was ignoring what lay ahead. I just didn't know how or where to start. I didn't have a plan, and I didn't know how to come up with one. I felt lost and adrift, along with a lot of other people who were in the same boat I was.

You know how frustrating it is to be incapable of reaching a worthwhile goal. You want to climb the ladder of success, but you can't even find the ladder. It's a lousy feeling.

I finally made up my mind that I didn't want to feel lousy any longer. I wanted to turn my dreams, goals, and ambitions into reality. I wanted to get from point A, where I was, to point B, where I wanted to be. So I learned how to plan.

For several years I was a management consultant for colleges and universities. I taught administrators how to plan everything from daily operations to annual budgets. They discovered that planning wasn't nearly as hard as they first thought. I think you'll discover the same thing.

I've tried to put everything I know about planning into this crisp, clear, and comprehensive book. It's just the thing to get you out of those starting blocks and on the fast track to success.

So, On your mark . . . Get set . . . . GO!

James R. Sherman, Ph.D.

INTRODUCTION

"A journey of a thousand miles begins with a single step."

You can bet your bottom dollar that when the Chinese philosopher Lao Tzu coined that phrase he didn't just vault over the top of the Great Wall and take off. Anyone traveling a thousand miles—or ten miles—should have some idea of where they're headed. If they don't, they're going to end up like Alice in Wonderland.

"Cheshire-Puss,". . . said Alice, "would you tell me, please, which way I ought to go from here?"

"That depends a good deal on where you want to get to," said the Cat.

"I don't much care where. . . " said Alice.

"Then it doesn't matter which way you go," said the Cat.

". . . so long as I get *somewhere*," Alice added as an explanation.

"Oh, you're sure to do that," said the Cat, "if you only walk long enough."

Alice doesn't seem to be too concerned about the fact that she doesn't know where life is taking her. But that's not the way you feel. Because if it were, you wouldn't be reading this book. You know you want something better than what you have right now, and you're frustrated because you don't know how to get it.

Frustration puts a damper on everything you do. It slows your progress to a crawl, breeds anxiety and despair, and bogs you down in the slough of despond. If you don't break out of its grip, with a plan to follow and a goal to pursue, you're destined to go through life as confused as Alice in Wonderland.

If you want to be successful, you have to find out where you are, de-

1

cide where you want to go, figure out what you have to do to get there, and then accomplish your goal with the fewest possible problems.

Those are simple planning steps, but a lot of folks find them difficult to carry out.

Planning holds the promise of a successful future. All you have to do to reap its rewards is execute a few basic planning tasks. Then instead of running around like a chicken with its head cut off, you'll be marching off to the land of milk and honey.

Planning is a proven method for achieving success, but it will only work for you if you want it to. If you're completely satisfied with your current level of productivity and think planning is a waste of time, then go no further. This book is not for you.

But if you feel angry, frustrated, and depressed, and if your days pass by with few, if any, significant results, then pay close attention to what follows. It will free you from your Alice-In-Wonderland existence and get you moving toward a bountiful future.

Start now by taking a look at the definition of planning.

THE DEFINITION OF PLANNING

Planning is the design of a hoped-for future and the development of effective steps for bringing it about.

Planning is a rational, systematic method of decision making and problem solving that combines experience, knowledge, and skill with realistic assessments of where you are and where you'd like to be.

Planning unveils the risks involved in charting a course into an unknown future. It helps you identify opportunities and threats that affect your chances of success and shows you how to utilize them to achieve hoped-for goals and objectives within specified periods of time. It guides you in the development and implementation of specific strategies for reaching critical milestones on the road to success. It makes you think ahead in terms of facts instead of fantasies. It gives you the power to control your future.

Planning helps you become the kind of person you really want to be.

Planning begins when you decide you want to do better than you're doing right now. It picks up speed as you collect data and develop alternative strategies. It gets into high gear when you choose a course of action and carry out a series of well-defined tasks. It reaches its climax when you achieve your sought-after level of success.

THE NATURE OF PLANNING

Effective planning is open-minded and flexible. It encourages change and modification, clarifies your image of reality, and enhances your visions of the future. It gauges your chances of success by telling you how far and how fast you need to go to reach a goal you really want. The promise it holds is fantastic.

There are two major types of planning. One deals with the future, the other with the here-and-now.

Future planning considers events that haven't happened yet, like a new job, a serious illness, a change in the weather, or the arrival of a baby. You can't always control these events, but through careful planning, you can deal with them more effectively if and when they happen.

Here-and-now planning deals with changes in your present circumstances, like losing weight, getting rid of a bad habit, taking a vacation, or starting a new relationship. You can control these events and effect the change you want by developing a here-and-now plan of action.

Besides these two types of planning, there are a couple of different ways in which planning is done. One is called *follow the leader planning*, where you try to copy what others have done in the past. The other approach is called *analytical planning*. You study a problem, check out alternative courses of action, and select what you think is the most promising solution.

Now you're really getting into the thick of it. Here are some additional planning concepts.

PLANNING MODELS

Planning models are miniature representations of what goes on in the real world. They give you a mind's eye view of what the planning process is all about.

Planning models provide the framework around which you can build any plan, no matter how complicated or long-lasting it might be. It can be a large corporate plan or a simple day-to-day plan for satisfying personal goals. Once you get accustomed to a planning framework, you can apply the model to anything.

This book follows the *inside-out* planning model. It's called inside-out because the primary focus is on you, the individual. Conversly, an *outside-in* model focuses on the world around you. You come second. Here's a brief description of both models.

Inside-out planning is tailored to what you're doing now and what you're able to do in the future. The process teaches you to focus on things you're good at and enjoy doing. It encourages you to do what's possible, instead of taking chances on hypothetical estimates of the world around you.

Inside-out planning lets you figure out what you personally need to do to reach your short-range and long-term goals and objectives. It calls for a lot of self-appraisal, which makes the process more reliable, because the qualities that describe you as an individual are more substantial and last longer than the qualities that describe the world you live in.

Outside-in planning, on the other hand, makes use of what other people think is happening now or is going to happen in the future. It calls for a continuous analysis of outside trends, conditions, and other environmental factors.

Companies that do outside-in planning will wait to hear the latest economic forecasts instead of going with what they know about their own economic condition. Individuals will postpone future events until someone else tells them that the time is ripe.

Outside-in planning causes time lags because it can only make use of information that other people have accumulated and are willing to provide. So if you're going to use the outside-in model, you'll have to wait until you can get access to the information you need.

The steps you take in the planning process are generally the same for all types and models. Those listed below are endorsed by most planning experts and are tailored to an inside-out approach.

THE SEVEN BASIC STEPS OF PLANNING

1. *Assessment:* You get an uneasy feeling about who you are and what you're doing. You see where you are in life and recognize a need—as well as a desire—to change.

2. *Commitment:* The need for change leads to a commitment on your part to accomplish that change. You recognize that planning is the way to go and you set aside time to do it.

3. *Investigation:* You study every aspect of your life, especially your history of successes and failures. You make a list of the skills you have to offer and the handicaps you have to bear. You examine the personal relationships you've had, especially those in which you've had to compete against others to get ahead. You figure out how much time you're going to have available for planning and you total up the benefits you're going to receive. Finally, you identify the risks you're going to have to take to bring about the change you want.

4. *Decision:* You get a gut feeling of what you think is going to happen in the future. Then, applying your intuition to everything you've learned, you come up with some alternative choices of what you want to do and when you want to do it.

5. *Organization:* You select the goals and objectives that are best suited to your needs and the planning strategy that will do the best job of getting you where you want to go. You set priorities, establish timetables, and figure out how you're going to evaluate your progress.

6. *Preparation:* You gather up everything you need to carry out your plan of action, including the suggestions found in this book. You fine-tune your plan and get ready to deal with any unforeseen circumstances.

7. *Implementation:* Once you start carrying out your plan, you need to pause from time to time to see how well your performance is measuring up against your original expectations. If you run into problems, you have to stop, change direction, and develop alternative ways of reaching your goals and objectives.

Is it all worth it? You bet it is.

THE BENEFITS OF PLANNING

Planning has so many benefits it's hard to mention them all. Here are some that really stand out.

1. *Gives Direction:* Planning makes you think about the promise of the future rather than the failures of the past.
2. *Coordinates:* Planning coordinates your drive to success by tying all activities together in a well-balanced program.
3. *Provides Standards:* Planning helps you set performance standards against which you can measure your progress and tell how well you're doing.
4. *Clarifies:* Planning clarifies what you want out of life by helping you establish clear-cut goals and objectives.
5. *Prepares:* Planning lets you see where sudden and unexpected problems are coming from and tells you how to anticipate and deal with them.
6. *Reveals:* Planning gives you a picture of how different tasks and activities interact to ensure success in your overall quest.
7. *Stimulates:* Planning leads you onward and upward, providing the stimulation you need to avoid dead-ends and blind alleys in work, creativity, and personal relationships.

Planning makes you more efficient and effective. It improves your morale, your attitudes, and your relationships with other people. You always know you're on the right track, and that gives you a sense of security about the days ahead.

The benefits of planning almost sound too good to be true. Once you get started, you'll find that it's everything it's cut out to be. But like every potent remedy, it can still cause problems if you're not careful. Here are some pitfalls to watch out for.

DANGERS IN PLANNING

No process is foolproof. And even when you think you've done everything right, you can still run into problems. Fortunately, none of the following dangers are so serious that they will sidetrack you completely.

1. *Loss of Spontaneity:* Spontaneity comes with flexibility. It means taking advantage of spur-of-the moment opportunities as soon as they happen. You can't plan to be spontaneous, that's a contradiction in terms. But you can plan to be flexible, and that's the key.

If your planning strategies are flexible, you'll gain spontaneity, encounter a wealth of opportunities, and have smooth sailing in your drive to success.

2. ***Too Much Faith in the Process:*** If you put too much faith in your plans, you may be afraid to break out and try something new. Your blind faith will keep you from seeing obstacles and alternatives that could effect your chances for success. Instead of moving ahead, you'll get shut down completely and your plans will come to a grinding halt.

3. ***Lack of Growth:*** You need the excitement and stimulation of new ideas, new knowledge, and new methods to ensure growth and accomplishment. Without growth, you'll stagnate. So no matter how good your plans seem when you first start out, you still have to allow for change and alteration or you'll end up high and dry.

4. ***Psychological Distress:*** Undisciplined planning can lead to short-sightedness, a lack of creativity, and an inability to innovate. And that can leave you as frustrated and unhappy as having no plans at all.

5. ***Hang-Up on Methods:*** If *how* it's done becomes more important than *if* it's done, then methods, techniques, and procedures will gradually take over the entire goal-seeking process and your dreams for the future will fade like a summer romance.

As you can see, the benefits in planning still far outweigh the dangers. By keeping an open mind and not allowing yourself to become addicted to the process, you can avoid these and other dangers entirely.

THERE'S MORE TO COME

You took two very significant steps when you saw a need to plan your future and committed yourself to being involved with the process. Lots of people never get that far, so you're already way ahead of the pack. When you get into section two, you'll see why many of these people will never be able to catch up.

Section three provides twenty-two specific guidelines for making sure your planning efforts turn out the way you want them to. By the time you get through all of them, you'll be in the backstretch, heading for home.

The last section gives you eight separate strategies for setting your plans in motion and carrying them out in the best way possible. By the time you finish the book, you'll have everything you need to plan a happy and prosperous future.

WHY PEOPLE DON'T PLAN

Planning takes lots of hard work and mental aerobics. You have to know where you are in life, what options are open to you, where you want to go, and what you have to do to get there. That requires self-examination and a thorough analysis of your strengths, weaknesses, thoughts, and feelings.

Maybe the thought of all that hard work is what makes some people doers instead of planners. Doers think it's a waste of time to try to figure out what's going to happen in a distant, hazy future. They would rather rely on the mysteries of chance to bring them success. But what they fail to recognize is that no one who has relied on chance alone has ever been consistently successful.

Chance is the assumed, impersonal, purposeless determiner of unaccountable happenings. It's pure chance when a coconut falls out of a palm tree and lands unnoticed in the sand. But if the coconut landed on your head, you'd consider that bad luck, and you'd be right.

Luck is chance that has been affected by human emotions. You can't influence chance, but you can affect the way you respond to it. If no one was around to see or hear the coconut fall, it would merely be a chance occurence. But if you saw the coconut fall and jumped out of the way to avoid it, you could say you were lucky.

The planning process helps shape your luck by showing you how to respond to falling coconuts and other external chances of life. You can, through careful planning, improve your potential for good luck and enhance your chance of success. You do it by recognizing good fortune whenever it occurs and by applying yourself to the opportunities it presents. If you don't respond to chance in a predetermined fashion, you run the risk of having bad luck or no luck at all.

People who rely on chance for their success always seem to come up short. And it isn't only their response to the vagaries of nature that clouds their future. Much of their misfortune lies in their dogged determination not to plan. Here are some of the major reasons why they choose to go this route.

BAD ATTITUDES

People who refuse to plan, or who are forced to do it against their wishes, are eager to say why it doesn't work. The attitudes they have toward planning help them rationalize their lack of success.

"Planning is too time consuming. I've got better things to do."

"There's too much work involved in planning. It's not worth the effort."

"The future is too unpredictable for planning to have any value. You can't see into the future, so why try to plan for it."

"I don't understand the planning process, and I won't waste my time learning something I can't use."

"We should live for today and not think about the future. What's happening now is more important than what might happen tomorrow."

"People should live by intuition and not by planning. I've got a gut feeling that what I'm doing is all right, and that takes care of all my planning needs."

ORNERYNESS

Stubbornness in the face of conflicting evidence almost always guarantees failure. It's a trait frequently found in people who, because of their jobs or some other reason, are drawn into the process against their will. They resent having to plan because someone told them to. Many of them deliberately set out to submarine the planning process as a singleminded way of asserting their individuality. It also gives them a means of avoiding responsibility if the planning process ever comes up short.

EXCESSIVE OPTIMISM

People who are overly optimistic see no reason to plan because they expect the future to be just as rosy as the present. They ignore threats, discard bad news when they hear it, and refuse to deal with obstacles that are staring them in the face. Their excessive zeal, need for immediate gratification, and inability to distinguish reality from fantasy misleads them into believing that life is always going to be a piece of cake.

These hopeful dreamers lack the foresight they need to adjust to unanticipated problems. They have not disciplined themselves to plan ahead, so they're generally unable to respond when their house of cards starts falling apart.

LACK OF PERCEPTION

People who can't see where they are, where they want to go, or what they have to do to reach their goals and objectives lack the perception they need to identify their strengths and weaknesses and the obstacles and contingencies that threaten their growth and development. They're left out of the planning process because they can't see what they have to do to get ahead.

Some of them divide their world into such small segments that they can no longer see it in its proper context. They interpret the world according to their own biased notions because they can't make heads or tails of what other people have told them. They're left with pieces of a puzzle that they can't put back together. So they eliminate several planning options that might otherwise lead to successful outcomes.

Many of these people are so saturated with random information, and so confused about what they're trying to do, that they fail to see the changes that are happening all around them. When they finally see where they are in life, they're too mixed up to shift gears or start over with a long-range plan.

INTELLECTUAL AND EXPRESSIVE BUGS

Some people don't plan because they can't muster the knowledge and skill they need to chart a course from the present to the future. They find it difficult to identify obstacles or to defuse them before they cause problems. Others don't have the tools that are needed to solve problems even after they've been recognized. And because many of these people have not been taught the basic elements of planning, they're unable to express their problems in ways that would lead to good solutions.

It's like someone not realizing that their house is on fire. And even when they discover that it is, they still don't know how to call for help.

INFLEXIBILITY

Some people not only ignore the benefits of planning, but also the knowledge that other people have gained from the planning process. In most cases their hopes for success have fallen short because they have insulated themselves from the advice, suggestions, and counsel of people who share their common experiences.

Nobody can hope to know and understand every detail that might affect them in the future. The world is just too complex. You do the best you can with what you're able to absorb and understand. But those who choose to chart their own course, while at the same time ignoring the experience of those who have gone before, have no one to blame but themselves for their lack of growth and development.

PROBLEMS WITH URGENCY

A fundamental principle of successful planning is to give highest priority to tasks that have the greatest importance. People who set their priorities according to urgency instead of importance never plan ahead, because they're too busy putting out fires. They're so wrapped up in trying to solve short-term crises that they seldom get a chance to work on their long-term goals. And it's usually the urgent need of someone else that seems to get most of the attention.

A parent sets aside an important task to tend to the urgent needs of a child. A worker sets aside an important task to handle a request that a manager wants completed as soon as possible. No sooner do these people commit themselves to someone else's urgent task, than they think of a better way to do the important task that they've just set aside. By then they're too committed to the urgent task to start over on the important task, so they usually wind up with lousy results in both areas. They wish they could do the important task over again, but there's no chance to do so because they've allowed another crisis to work its way to the top, and the cycle continues.

The only way these people are going to reach their hoped-for levels of success is by establishing a plan that allows them to reach their own goals and still handle other people's urgent needs on a contingency basis.

SOCIAL TABOOS AND ENVIRONMENTAL BLOCKS

Social taboos are what keep people from walking around naked when their air-conditioners are busted. Environmental blocks are what keep people from taking advantage of opportunities that exist outside their own life space in different neighborhoods, whether in small towns, big cities, little companies, large corporations, or foreign countries.

Traditions, social customs, and regional folklore often keep people from adapting to the changing nature of their world or from coming up with a variety of ways of preparing for their future. People who give in to social taboos or environmental blocks can't plan ahead because they're unable or unwilling to adapt to new surroundings or to accept new standards of behavior. They often respond to new cultures or environments by saying, "That's not the way I do things," or "That's not the way I've been brought up."

LIMITED VIEWPOINTS

Some people don't plan because they don't like to try new, untested methods or venture into unfamiliar territory. They prefer to live in the present, doing what they've always done and are most comfortable with. They're ready to judge new ideas, but not generate them. They sometimes sense a need to change, but they'll usually back away from doing anything about it if they think there could be problems involved. They don't have a very good idea of what their strengths and weaknesses are because they've never been tested against adversity. If they've had any success in the past, it's only because they've been doing the same things over and over again.

Until these people are willing to venture beyond their limited horizons, their hopes for success will remain unfulfilled and they'll spend most of their time mired in mediocrity.

FEAR OF THE UNKNOWN

People who nurture an overriding desire for security and order, and an intolerance for chaos, are afraid of an ambiguous and unknown future and the risk of potential failure. They refuse to program their lives around planning assumptions because there is no guarantee that those assumptions will turn out the way they want them to. They're so obsessed with surviving in the present that they never have time to prepare for the future. They would rather stick with current operating routines and avoid the possibility of making a mistake.

LACK OF PERSEVERANCE

Some people can't stick to a course of action, no matter how well it's spelled out. They give up easily when faced with even the slightest obstacle or distraction.

Others will develop a plan of action and commit themselves so firmly to it that they will resist all distractions and do everything they can to accomplish their intended goal.

The difference between people who plan and people who don't is as explainable as the difference in people's ability to solve intellectual problems or perform acts of skill.

People who recognize their shortcomings, but who still want to succeed in life, don't let themselves get discouraged whenever they run into difficulties. They just do the best they can and try to get better at what they're doing.

THE KEY INGREDIENTS

There is, and always will be, a significant difference between people who find success in planning and those who choose to remain a step behind. The biggest difference can be found in the personality traits that characterize successful planners.

1. *Curiosity*: Good planners take time to figure out why things are as they seem to be. They seek answers to questions about the future and their chances for success.

2. *Creativity*: Good planners look for new ideas or new ways of applying old ideas to day-to-day activities.
3. *Competitiveness*: Good planners enjoy intellectual competition and
   are skilled at verbal give-and-take. They look for strengths and
   weaknesses in other people's ideas and test contradictory positions
   against their own.
4. *Practicality*: Good planners are realistic, enthusiastic, and very
   pragmatic about their chances for success. They know what can be
   done, how fast it can be completed, and what they have to do to
   finish it.
5. *Confidence*: Good planners can cope with criticism and rejection
   from any quarter. Logic and reason help them persevere no matter
   what the odds.
6. *Wisdom*: Good planners keep up with developments in all fields of
   knowledge, especially those that effect their goals and objectives.
7. *Persistence*: Good planners are so committed to their well-turned
   plans that they're able to overcome just about any obstacle or threat
   that stands in their way.

If you think you lack any of the traits that characterize successful
planners, do what you can to add them to your repertoire. It'll keep you
from getting discouraged when you run into seemingly impossible
problems.

You should also spend as much time as you can trying to understand
the relationship between chance, luck, and planning.

CHANCE AND PLANNING

Chance is is made up of an infinite number of unforeseeable happenings, both great and small, that are constantly taking place in the world
around us. Chance events happen unexpectedly, without discernible human intervention or observable cause. They cannot be planned, predicted,
or prearranged.

With more and more people living in less and less space, and moving
about more rapidly than ever, there are bound to be more unpredictable
encounters, more strange coincidences, and more fortuitous opportunities

than ever before. And the more chances there are, the more good luck you'll be able to get out of them.

Some people are affected more by chance than others. It doesn't take much imagination to figure out how chance and luck might affect the lives of a canoe outfitter in the north woods of Minnesota and a commodities broker on the Chicago Board of Trade.

The outfitter and the broker see themselves differently in terms of their strengths, weaknesses, threats, and opportunities. An unpredictable change in the weather may have a marginal effect on the outfitter. But the broker may see it as having a significant impact on future commodity prices. A nuisance bear may not concern the broker, but it could affect the way the outfitter deals with people who expect to take a pleasant trip into the wilderness.

You cannot know the cause of everything that happens around you, nor can you accurately predict the occurrence of every event that might affect your future. But you can make some educated guesses. And once you've made those guesses, you can make plans to encounter chance events if and when they happen.

Success doesn't happen by chance. It comes from hard work and planning. If successful people seem lucky, it's because they plan ahead to take advantage of every opportunity that comes their way.

THE PLAY GOES ON

By now you should have a good understanding of the planning process and of all the advantages and disadvantages that go with it. And you should understand why some people choose not to plan. You should also have a pretty good idea of the promise that planning holds for your future. What you need now are some tips on how to put it all together. That's coming up next.

Section three starts out with six preliminary concepts that will get you primed for planning. Then you'll be introduced to eighteen specific techniques that will help you get through the planning process.

Section four will show you how to put it all together into a plan of action that will send you forward on the pathway to success.

HOW TO PLAN

You've been introduced to some of the fundamentals of planning, and you've encountered a number of reasons why some short-sighted people choose not to plan. Now you're probably all set to do some planning of your own. But before you get involved with a major project, you should run through a few preliminary concepts to give yourself a better base from which to start. Here are some thoughts about risk, luck, contingencies, assumptions, performance measures, and endings.

THE ELEMENT OF RISK

Risk is the measured possibility of experiencing a loss, an injury, or some other unfavorable outcome. You face calculated risks every day of your life in everything you do, including the risk of being in an auto accident, of catching a cold, or of losing money in the stock market. If you hope to be successful, you have to know something about your risks and your chances of success. You especially need to know how much risk you can afford and still be comfortable with what you're doing.

Let's assume that your project consists of five separate events, each of which has an 80-percent chance of success. That means that for any single event, you have two chances in ten of getting unfavorable results.

That sounds pretty good, but it may surprise you to know that *your chance of success for all five events taken together is not 80 percent, but 33 percent, or one in three.*

Figuring out your chance of success for a planned project that is made up of several events is fairly simple. You multiply the odds of the first event by the odds of the second event by the odds of the third event, on down the line. In this case, multiplying 80 percent (.80) by itself five times turns out to be 33 percent (.33). In order to increase the probability of your five-event project to 80 percent, you'd have to increase the probability of success for each event to almost 96 percent.

Obviously, a simple plan, where only a few things can go wrong, will have a much better chance of being successful than one with several independent events. But no matter what the odds are, you'll still be a lot better off by planning than you would be if you cast your lot to the winds and hoped for the best.

LUCK AND PLANNING

You can improve your luck and enhance your prospects of being successful by understanding the interplay between external chance and inward response.

A chance event, like meeting a stranger or discovering a new piece of information, can shape your luck and determine your success, but it will not affect you unless you respond to it. Your response will be determined in large part by your needs, attitudes, and patterns of behavior that have evolved throughout your lifetime.

The more you know about what you really want and the better prepared you are, the better you'll be at applying yourself when a favorable chance appears. And the more chances you have, the more good luck you'll be able to get out of them.

The secret lies in planning; the process of identifying the strengths, interests, and personal qualities you would like to develop and in applying those characteristics whenever you get an opportunity to do so.

Planning will help you maintain a high level of readiness. You'll recognize good fortune when it appears, you'll take advantage of the opportunity it presents, and you'll experience a tremendous surge of fulfillment that will stay with you for a long time to come.

PLANNING FOR CONTINGENCIES

A contingency is something that is possible but uncertain. No one can say for sure if it will happen or not. When it does occur, it usually comes when least expected. A flat tire, an unexpected guest, or a broken water heater are all examples of contingencies.

Contingencies can completely immobilze people who are tied to complicated and unresponsive plans. Their fixed schedules don't allow for spontaneous actions when the inevitable monkey wrench gets thrown in the works.

Contingencies can be devastating. But you can still plan for them in spite of their uncertain nature, and either avoid them or get through them without any trouble.

Contingency plans don't have to be elaborate. Having a spare tire in your car qualifies. So does a well-balanced investment plan. Just follow the old adage of not putting all your eggs in one basket.

One good thing about having a contingency plan is that its very existence and the approach it implies help guarantee that you'll never need it. Your awareness of potential problems keeps you in a state of readiness that usually prevents contingencies from actually happening.

Contingencies can sometimes enhance a planned course of action, especially when they force you to come up with creative solutions to the problems they create. The demands these spontaneous outbursts put on you can enrich your understanding of the planning process and increase your chances for a successful outcome.

PLANNING ASSUMPTIONS

A planning assumption is something you think is true and can be taken for granted. It's a gut feeling you have about what you think is going to happen in the next few weeks, months, or years. Planning assumptions are based on investigative findings that relate to you and the world you live in. These assumptions can involve anything you think will have an impact on your life, including economic conditions, anticipated business developments, or changes in your social life. They are the foundation upon which you develop the goals and objectives of your plan.

PERFORMANCE MEASURES

You've probably asked yourself from time to time whether or not you're heading in the right direction. Or you've wondered, after reaching a goal, if you've been successful or not.

Sometimes it's easy to see what you've done. You've lost 15 pounds or you haven't. You've saved $1500 or you haven't. You've gotten your promotion or you haven't. These objectives are fairly easy to measure. But you're not going to know if your plans are falling into place or not if you don't have some way of measuring your performance. So *before* you start to implement your plan, be sure you know what you're going to measure and how you're going to do it.

Here are some criteria you can use to develop performance measures that will tell you how well you're doing in carrying out your plan.

1. Your previous history of success and failure. (Are you doing better or worse than you've done in the past?)
2. Levels of achievement you think are possible. (How much, how many, how far, how long?)
3. Expectations of people who are evaluating you, and your feelings about those evaluations. (What are you expected to do and for whom?)
4. Actual progress, as measured by facts and figures. (Pounds, dollars, grades, points)
5. The cost in time and other resources needed to reach your goals and objectives. (Are the benefits more or less than the costs?)

Let's say that you're planning to increase your sales from $75,000 to $100,000. What measures of success would you use? Number of dollars, rapport with customers, respect of your colleagues, admiration from your family, or all of the above? How would you measure these outcomes against the sacrifices you'd have to make, like spending more time away from home or going head-to-head in direct competition with a friend?

The best measure of success is your self-image, which is the set of values you hold for yourself. Are you proud of your accomplishments? Have you gained increased feelings of self-worth by sticking to your plan and reaching your goals and objectives? What is your status among the groups and individuals that are important to you?

ENDINGS

There is only one ending in life. So one of the most important things you can learn when making plans is to give up the concept of a perfect ending. If you don't, your quest for a simple, happy outcome will end in frustration.

Life is not simple, it's complex. That's why it's fun. To get the most out of life, you need to think of it as a long, never-ending pathway, stretching far ahead, with lots of other pathways leading off to either side. The pathway you choose will be determined by your goals and objectives and the success you have in carrying out your plans.

You might never arrive at the goal you originally set. Or if you do, you'll probably see it in a different light, and another goal will spring up that will seem more important. You might, as an example, set out to get a college degree. But as that goal comes closer to reality, it will no longer be thought of as the end of your journey. It will become a milestone toward another goal like getting a job, starting a family, or going to graduate school.

Each new goal will bring with it the challenge and excitement of a chase. There will be new stars to shoot for and new dreams of things to come. That's what makes life fun and keeps you growing.

The following list of strategies will help get you ready to plan, show you the difference between good and bad planning, and give you the tools you need to reach your goals and objectives.

1. QUIZ YOURSELF

Answers to each of the following questions will help you develop a clear picture of where you are now and what you want to do in the future.

1. What are the most significant events that have happened to you in the past three to five years. Why do you think they're important? What is your record of successes and failures?
2. What's your position in the world today? How well are you performing? What results can you expect from your present activities? What have you sown and what will you reap?
4. What do you want to be? Where do you want to go? What are your goals and objectives? What is your philosophy of life?
5. How are you going to get where you want to go? What tools and resources are you going to need to get there? What should you change? What should you keep the same?

6. How will you know when you've completed the milestones you've identified?

Your answers will not only give you a better understanding of your capabilities and limitations, they'll also give you a realistic idea of some of the opportunities that are open to you.

You can broaden your perspective, enhance your planning activities, and improve your chances of success even more by getting additional information from friends, relatives, loved ones, and business associates.

2. DETERMINE YOUR STRENGTHS

The is the first exercise you need to complete as you start developing your plans for the future.

Take a sheet of paper like that shown on the next page and draw a line across the middle. On the top half, write down all the *things you're good at*; deeds you've done that have earned you praise from other people or have given you a lot of self-satisfaction. List things like making money, speaking in public, playing a musical instrument, taking part in sporting events, building objects with your hands, or selling products or ideas to other people. Include intangible strengths like values, self-esteem, work attitudes, willingness to accept risk, and other attributes that set you apart from the crowd. Be objective. Don't put down qualities you just wish you had, and don't ignore characteristics you think are not important.

On the bottom half of the sheet, put down *things you enjoy doing* whether you're good at them or not; things like hiking, camping, traveling, playing tennis, managing money, closing a sale, completing a report, or meeting new people.

The areas of strength that are going to have the greatest impact on your future success are those that are related to your health, intelligence, experiences, motivation, personal appearance, and talents and skills.

If you can concentrate on doing things you're good at and enjoy, your chances of success will increase tremendously.

3. DETERMINE YOUR WEAKNESSES

This exercise is just as important as the last one, so give it just as much attention.

MY LIST OF STRENGTHS

Things I'm Good At

_____

_____

_____

_____

_____

_____

_____

Things I Like To Do

_____

_____

_____

_____

_____

_____

_____

Divide another sheet of paper like you did before. On the top half, put down activities that *you're not very good at* or that you just can't seem to develop a knack for doing. Personal habits like laziness, indifference, lack of concentration, and inability to communicate can all affect your planning success, so be sure to include them as weaknesses. But don't put down things like mountain climbing or sailboat racing if you've never done them before.

On the bottom half of the page, put down *things you don't like to do*, like getting up early, writing up sales reports, staying in the office, or talking on the telephone. Put down anything you'd avoid doing if you could.

Include physical as well as mental shortcomings that keep you from moving ahead. And be honest with yourself. It's better to identify problem areas before you get started than to discover them after you're hopelessly locked in an impossible journey.

You might be very good at something you don't enjoy doing, or you may enjoy doing something for which you have no talent. You're more inclined to develop a skill for something you like to do than for something you don't like. So if you like something, list it among your strengths, and if you don't like it, put it down with your weaknesses.

Weaknesses that involve interactions with family, friends, business associates, and social contacts can all affect your ability to succeed. Include them wherever you can.

You've probably already figured out that if you can avoid doing things you don't like to do or are not very good at, you'll have a much better chance of being successful.

4. ITEMIZE OPPORTUNITIES AND THREATS

The mental aerobics continue.

Take another sheet of paper and on the top half, write down every idea, situation, or circumstance you can think of that might help you be successful. If your competition is weak and you are strong, put that down as an opportunity. If you're doing something you enjoy and are good at, put that down on the same list. Include intangible opportunities, like your reputation, the area in which you live, or your relationships with other people.

On the bottom half of the page, write down anything you can think

LIST OF WEAKNESSES

Things I'm Not Very Good At

_____

_____

_____

_____

_____

_____

Things I Don't Like To Do

_____

_____

_____

_____

_____

_____

OPPORTUNITIES I HAVE

_____

_____

_____

_____

_____

_____

_____

THREATS I FACE

_____

_____

_____

_____

_____

_____

_____

_____

of that might frustrate your efforts, slow down your progress, or sidetrack your drive for success. Include in this list of threats your competition if it's stronger than you, your lack of expertise if you're just starting out, or a small clientele if you're in a highly competitive business.

5. COMPARE YOUR LISTS

Now you've got four lists of what you think are strengths, weaknesses, opportunities and threats. The next step is to combine the items on those lists in a way that will help you plan your future and reach your dreams of success.

Combine your strengths, which are the things you like to do and are good at, with your list of opportunities. Figure out which opportunities exist because of your strengths and which strengths exist only because of the opportunities you have available. Those are the combinations you'll want to work on the most because they have the greatest potential for growth and improvement.

An opportunity may exist because you lack competition, have a lot of customers, and carry a good product line. Combine that opportunity with your willingness to work hard and your ability to sell things to other people, and you'll increase your chances of being a successful salesperson. Opportunities and strengths will always work to your advantage if you recognize their relationship and can capitalize on it.

Now combine the things you don't like to do, or tend to screw up from time to time, with your list of threats. Some threats will exist only because of your weaknesses, and some weaknesses will exist only because of threats you've identified. Flag those combinations because they can cause some of your worst difficulties.

Imagine someone who faces the threat of not being able to move ahead in their job. Combine that with their weakness of not having a college degree and their lack of time and money needed to go back to school. Add their difficulty in taking examinations and their inability to concentrate on difficult tasks. You can already see that a combination like that is not going to generate much success. They'd be better off looking for another job or trying to develop some new skills.

Don't try to match your list of strengths against your list of threats. And don't try to take advantage of an opportunity by doing things you

MY COMBINATION OF
OPPORTUNITIES AND STRENGTHS

MY COMBINATION OF
THREATS AND WEAKNESSES

_____

_____

_____

_____

_____

_____

_____

_____

_____

_____

_____

_____

_____

_____

aren't good at or don't like to do. Concentrate instead on combining your strengths with obvious opportunities, while avoiding combinations of weaknesses and threats. If you're successful at this, you'll spend 80 to 90 percent of your time doing what you want to do in situations that are going to help you, and only 10 to 20 percent of your time doing things you don't enjoy doing or aren't very good at.

Go over your lists of weaknesses and threats from time to time and see where you can avoid or eliminate them altogether, especially where they work together to keep you from being successful.

6. KNOW WHAT YOU WANT TO DO

If you don't know where you're going, you'll probably end up someplace else.

Write down every success-generating, strength/opportunity idea you come up with no matter how farfetched it may seem when it first comes to mind. Give it serious consideration because sudden and spontaneous insight and seat-of-the-pants ideas can be very productive. Follow your intuition but don't let it overrule objective decision making. If your newly-hatched idea fails to hold water, then discard it and open your mind again to other thoughts.

Rewrite general ideas as specific tasks that can be done right away. Tear into them without hesitation. They'll keep you from procrastinating and give you a good start on your trek to a successful future.

7. DEVELOP GOALS AND OBJECTIVES

Goals and objectives are the steppingstones to success and the footings upon which all planning is based. Without them, your hopes for a happy and prosperous future stand little chance of being fulfilled.

Goals are broad, long-term, idealistic statements of hoped- for accomplishments. Objectives are clear, concise statements of activities you want to complete in specific time periods. Your goal may be a wistful desire to lose an unspecified amount of weight. Your objective would be to start today to lose seven pounds within a three-week period. Objectives are almost always measured by how much, how far, how big, or how many. That makes it easier to tell whether they have been reached or not.

Goals and objectives should be realistic, attainable, challenging, and measurable. They should represent things you really want and are willing to work for. Goals and objectives can either be positive or negative, and they can either drive you toward something or away from it. If your goal is to lose weight, you may want to look slimmer (positive goal) or avoid looking fat (negative goal).

Life is dynamic, fluctuating, and always changing. So goals and objectives have to be flexible or they won't be of much use. If they're not renewed from time to time, they'll soon be out of date and lose their importance. If a goal is unreachable, back off and establish a more realistic outcome. If a goal looks too easy, raise your sights and try for something bigger.

Milestones are intermediate points you need to reach along the way toward meeting your overall objectives. If they're spaced close together, you'll arrive at them sooner and satisfy them quicker. That will boost your morale, give you a greater sense of accomplishment, and generate the enthusiasm you'll need to reach your final goal.

8. ESTABLISH YOUR CRITERIA

It's not easy to tell how successful you are in meeting your goals and objectives unless you have some standards upon which you can base your decisions.

Goals and objectives should be as specific as possible without being too restrictive. If you're going on a diet, say how many pounds you want to lose, don't just say you want to lose weight. If you're planning to reach a professional goal, spell it out so you know exactly what you're shooting for.

Avoid exaggerations, misconceptions, idealistic terms, oversimplifications, opinions that are subject to change, understated or overstated words, and terms that have a wide range of meaning. Use precise terms so you never have any doubts about what you're shooting for. But stay flexible so you can change your goals whenever it becomes necessary.

Make a list of the methods you're going to use and the resources you'll consume. Identify every reasonable course of action that's available to you. Weigh the advantages and disadvantages of each, then figure out which ones hold the most promise.

Translate your chosen course of action into a concise statement of what you're going to do and how, when, where, and why you're going to do it. If anyone should ask what you're up to, you should be able to respond in one clearly thought-out sentence. Write it down on a piece of paper and keep it in front of you so you're always aware of what you're trying to do. Attach it to your bathroom mirror, stick it on your refrigerator door, glue it to the dashboard of your car, or hang it over your desk.

9. MANAGE YOUR TIME

Time gives substance to your plans. It tells you when some things ought to be done, and it reminds you when it's too late to do others. If you don't have a calendar to guide your efforts, your plans will seem like meaningless wanderings through space.

Manage time like money. Keep track of what you use, and balance your calendar the way you balance your checkbook. Know how much you can do in a specified time period. Set aside prime time for the really important tasks. Maintain a tight schedule to keep from dawdling and procrastinating. Consolidate your efforts in the time you have, then watch your productivity go up.

Your deadlines should be precise but flexible. Overly ambitious deadlines can inspire you to greater efforts or they can cause you to take dangerous short cuts. Easy deadlines lead to procrastination. Indefinite deadlines are too easily ignored.

10. CLARIFY YOUR PLAN

Identify the major steps you have to take to reach your goals and objectives. If your plan is laid out clearly in front of you, you'll know where you've been, where you are, and where you're headed.

Streamline your plan so it's easy to follow. Avoid overlap, conflict, and duplication. Take shortcuts when you see them, and pass over any unnecessary tasks that get in your way. Be sure to have a contingency plan ready in case something goes wrong.

Schedule activities and events over different time periods so everything doesn't happen at once. Identify specific dates—days, weeks, months, years—on which milestones will be reached and objectives will be attained. Keep big and little achievements happening on a regular basis to add variety to your program.

The more short-term success you can generate, the more control you'll have over the whole planning process. So develop lots of day-to-day objectives where you have a good chance of being successful. Then build on these successful outcomes by incorporating your most productive methods into your long-range plans.

Determine what performance measures you're going to use to figure out if you've reached an objective and how well you did to get there.

11. PLAY THE ODDS

Planning and poker have a lot in common. They both call for decisions that are based on incomplete and sometimes inaccurate information and they're both affected by chance. You'll see a lot more success in your planning efforts if you know what your odds are before you start and are able to use them to your advantage.

What are your odds of winning a lottery? How do professors grade on a curve? What percentage of all marriages end in divorce? How many customers are in your territory and what are your odds of landing a sale over three other vendors?

Use analytic methods to examine your imaginative hunches. Concentrate on events where the odds are good, and avoid activities where success seems impossible. Accept as much risk as you can afford. Change your strategy whenever you think it will improve your odds.

12. ESTABLISH AND ASSIGN PRIORITIES

A task is important if it yields a high return for the time invested and clearly contributes to the achievement of your long-term goals and objectives. An urgent task is simply one that calls for immediate action. It could be a complete waste of time.

Go through your list of things to do and ask yourself if each task is moving you closer to a lifetime goal or if it's sending you off in the wrong direction. Put a star by the tasks that are directly related to your goals and then arrange them in order of priority, putting those that are important *and* urgent at the top of your list. Important, non-urgent tasks should have next highest priority. Start each day by doing those things that give you the most pleasure and provide the biggest payoff.

Sometimes it makes sense to work on a task that's not as urgent or important as another. If it doesn't take much time, and if the benefits are substantial, it could serve as a warm-up exercise for more important tasks.

Don't stop to establish priorities every time you're ready to begin a new task. Your day will be much more productive if you assign your priorities first thing in the morning or the night before you go to work. You'll be in better control of your time and you'll know that important things are being tended to.

Reexamine your priorities from time to time and feel free to change them if you have a good reason for doing so. Don't be afraid to say "no" to unimportant tasks that can disrupt your overall strategy. Keep your goals first and foremost in your mind so you don't get caught in the trap of overestimating the importance of what you're doing.

Make sure your priorities are realistic and well-suited to what you're trying to do. When you're standing knee-deep in alligators, it's hard to remember that you were supposed to clean the swamp.

13. PRIME THE PUMP

You can reach any goal faster and better if you can create in your mind's eye an image of yourself getting it done. The key lies in the intensity of your vision and the depth of your concentration.

Professional golfers, before they swing, try to get an image of their shot hitting the green and dropping in the cup. Downhill racers, before they compete, try to see themselves making every gate and crossing the finish line in record time.

The technique is called dynamic imaging and it can work as well for you as anyone. You just have to avoid overblown standards and unreasonable expectations and think only about realistic goals and objectives you know you can accomplish.

Picture yourself as an attractively thin person if you're trying to lose weight. Picture yourself in graduation garb if you're a struggling college student. See yourself as a happy spouse, a successful business person, or as anything else you'd like to be.

Your ability to recall visual stimuli is limited only by your imagination. You can enhance your vision even more by approaching your goals and objectives with all of your senses. Taste them, smell them, see them, hear them, and touch them if you can.

14. MAKE A COMMITMENT

Formalize your responsibilities in a commitment – to yourself and others – that you're going to follow through with your plan. Share your commitment with your spouse, parents, children, siblings, colleagues, a favorite mentor, or others who you trust and respect. They'll not only share your enthusiasm, they'll help determine your strengths and weaknesses, assess your progress, and evaluate your results.

Believe in what you're doing and in the goals you have selected to pursue. Establish a climate that's conducive to change. Innovate wherever you can. Concentrate on long-term goals but take pleasure in short-term accomplishments. Carry out your plan with vim, vigor, and vitality. Convince yourself that what you're about to embark on is what you really want to do and that you're fully capable of carrying it out.

Understand the theoretical concepts that are inherent in your plan as well as the psychological principles that support it. Be realistic about your projections and prepare to live up to your expectations.

15. START WHEN READY

Don't get so wrapped up in the process of planning that you fail to recognize when it's time to start moving. Make sure your first task is an easy one, especially if it's going to take a tremendous amount of energy for you to get out of the starting blocks. That first task should break the bonds of inertia, get you off dead center, and lead you right into the rest of your plan.

Don't worry about contingencies, meet them head-on when they first appear. If you find out later that you've made a mistake, admit it, back up, and start over. The worst thing you can do is sit still and procrastinate.

16. WORK AT IT

The only place where success comes before work is in the dictionary.

Recognize peak performance periods and use them for working on really tough tasks. Save routine work for less productive times. Prune back any unnecessary tasks that slow you down and distract you from your overall goal. Maintain a consistent level of effort and concentrate on what you're doing.

Success is habit forming. If you work hard at being good in one area of your life, your success will carry over into every other area you're involved in. You'll not only make tremendous progress, you'll be in a better position to handle any unexpected problems that might come up.

Take time, whenever you reach a milestone, to figure out where you are, what you've done to get there, and what you have to do to keep moving. Reflect on your list of tasks and see how well you did. Incorporate today's insights into tomorrow's plans.

Document any unexpected events that spring up along the way. Figure out what strategies work best and refer back to them whenever your progress is slowed or blocked. Gather a storehouse of information about your progress and use it where it will do the most good.

If you're like most people, you do 80 percent of your most productive work in 20 percent of the time you have available. That leaves plenty of time for adjustments and improvements. So fill in that extra time with special tasks. Build a sense of improvement into your expectations and work hard at doing better day by day.

17. STAY FLEXIBLE

Everything around you is changing, so even a well-drawn plan may be out of date by the time you put it to use. The only plan that's 100 percent up-to-date is one that's already in need of change.

Diversity is the best protection against catastrophe. So keep some alternative strategies ready in case your initial plan doesn't work out. Replace strategies that fail to live up to your expectations.

Keep analyzing the interaction between your strengths, weaknesses, opportunities, and threats, even after you've reached some preliminary goals and objectives. Stay flexible and keep thinking about what lies ahead. Postpone judgment of what's important and what's not until you reach the point where you can deal with new ideas without prejudice. It will be easier to come up with alternative courses of action if it looks like changes in strategy might be helpful.

Don't take spectacular leaps unless you're a trapeze artist. Recognize and use the power of patience. You'll see it in the flowering of a rose, the growing of a tree, and in many other events in nature. None of them happen all at once, they happen in bits and pieces over time.

18. KNOW YOUR WORLD

Look around you for critical ingredients of success and key factors of growth. They'll help you put together some realistic goals and objectives. Determine how economic and social factors can affect your outcomes. They may provide opportunities that you might otherwise overlook.

Recognize your leaders and describe the effect they have on your efforts. Compare your skills with those of your colleagues, competitors, and role models to see if you have what it takes to hold your own against the tide. See if you're operating at their level, doing better than they are, or trailing behind. Find out if they're doing things that you could do just as well. See if you can incorporate their techniques and strategies into your own plans for success.

Know how you relate to the individuals you work with or to those who are a part of your personal life. Are you the head honcho or just part of the crowd? Are there bigger or smaller fish in your pond? Size up your relationships with everyone who is going to have a significant impact on your designs for the future.

SUMMARY

Be physically and emotionally ready to set your plan in motion. Know what makes a good plan and a good planner. Recognize some of the probable causes of failure and know how to avoid them. Plan for the problems you hope will never come. And whenever opportunity knocks, be sure you're there to answer the door.

Now you're ready for action. In the next section you'll discover eight additional suggestions that will help you put your plan in operation. You'll also get another look at the seven basic steps of planning.

PLAN OF ACTION

You've designed your hoped-for future, and by spelling out your goals and objectives, you've taken the first few steps toward getting there. Now all you have to do is carry out your plan.

Decide what parts of your plan are most important and set out to do those first. Organize your tasks around a realistic timetable so you can get a better idea of what you have to do and when you have to do it. Figure out ways of measuring your performance so you'll be able to see how well you've done. And be sure you know what the odds are for coming out ahead of the pack.

Here are eight planning strategies that will help you get your planning efforts underway and lead you to a successful future.

1. *Develop The Planning Habit*: Plan everything you do until the process becomes automatic. Start with simple day-to-day errands, then work your way up to lifetime goals and objectives. Know which tasks are most important and do those first. Leave no more to chance than is absolutely necessary.

2. *Find A Place*: Your physical surroundings and the people around you should contribute to your planning efforts, not frustrate them. So find a place where you'll be encouraged to plan. Experiment with different settings. Work alone or with someone. Ask for suggestions, or keep to yourself. See what works best for you and utilize it as best you can.

3. *Delegate*: Know what you have to do to complete your tasks and know what kind of help you're going to need from others. Delegate

complete authority and responsibility to people who know what you're doing and are willing to help. Give them crystal-clear instructions, then back off and let them do the best they can.

4. *Be Accurate*: Base your plans on concrete facts and real situations. Know the difference between the way things are and the way you want them to be. Get the best information available, then draw up realistic estimates of your chances for success.

5. *Be Perceptive*: Be on the alert for new opportunities, and take advantage of them whenever you can. Anticipate obstacles and devise effective means of getting rid of them. Develop alternate plans to insure against contingencies. Know where you are every step of the way.

6. *Keep It Simple*: Your plan should be simple, well organized, and clearly understood. Tasks and activities should be well-defined, timetables should be realistic, and resources should be attainable.

7. *Get Better*: Don't leave planning to chance. If you don't have the skill, discipline, or expertise to carry out your plans, then take time to acquire them. Strive for greater competency through daily practice and additional study.

8. *Be Flexible*: Be responsive to every possibility. Modify, change, or revise your plans if they prove to be unworkable or obsolete. Avoid the functionally and psychologically destructive stress of inflexibility.

Back in section one you were introduced to the seven basic steps of the planning process. Here they are again in abbreviated form. They provide an excellent framework upon which you can develop everything you need for a plan of action.

1. *Assessment*: Figure out where you are now and where you want to be in the future. Clarify your need to be successful in whatever endeavors you choose to pursue.

2. *Commitment*: Cross you heart and hope to die that you'll go to work right now on a plan for the future.

3. *Investigation*: Take a look at yourself from every angle and write down what you find. Develop a profile of who you are and what you want to be.

4. *Decision*: Make up you mind about what you want to do and when you want to do it.
5. *Organization*: Develop some specific goals and objectives and set a timetable for carrying them out.
6. *Preparation*: Gather together all the resources you're going to need to carry out your plan of action.
7. *Implementation*: Launch a leading task that will put your plan in motion and follow up on everything you do.

The first step you take in carrying out a plan of action is often the most important one. It can help overcome the inertia that has held you back in the past and it can lead you into a continuous pattern of growth and development.

Turn to the next page where the seven basic steps of planning are listed and write down a leading task for each one. Make the leading tasks relatively easy so you don't have to put a lot of effort into them. Just make sure that each task is pertinent to the longterm goals you're hoping to achieve.

A FINAL WORD

When asked why he spent so much time in planning and thinking about the future, Charles Kettering, then chairman of General Motors, replied, "My interest is in the future because I'm going to spend the rest of my life there."

Today is the first day of the rest of your life. At this time tomorrow, you'll be one day short. Don't let any more days get away without filling them to the brim with productive activities.

Recognize the power in planning and the promise it holds for controlling your future. Have the courage and commitment to start planning today. Do it now, cuz time's a wasting.

On your mark. . . Get set. . . GO!

SEVEN STEPS TO A SUCCESSFUL FUTURE

1. **Assessment:**
   Leading task: _____

   _____

   _____

2. **Commitment:**
   Leading task: _____

   _____

   _____

3. **Investigation:**
   Leading task: _____

   _____

   _____

4. **Decision:**
   Leading task: _____

   _____

   _____

SEVEN STEPS TO A SUCCESSFUL FUTURE

5. Organization:
   Leading task: _____

   _____

   _____

6. Preparation:
   Leading task: _____

   _____

   _____

7. Implementation:
   Leading task: _____

   _____

   _____

GOOD LUCK!

INDEX

INDEX

—Notes—

—Notes—

—Notes—

—Notes—

—Notes—